The Listening Walk

by PAUL SHOWERS • illustrated by ALIKI

HOUGHTON MIFFLIN   BOSTON

The Listening Walk

I like to take walks.

I take walks with my father and our dog.

Our dog is called Major.

He is an old dog, and he does not walk very fast.

We go down the street, and we do not talk.

My father puts his hands in his pockets and thinks.

Major walks ahead and sniffs.

I keep still and listen.

I call this a Listening Walk.

On a Listening Walk I do not talk.

I listen to all the different sounds.

I hear many different sounds when I do not talk.

First I hear Major's toenails on the sidewalk.

Major has long toenails.

When he walks, his toenails scratch the sidewalk.

They go *twick twick twick twick*.

I hear my father's shoes on the sidewalk.

My father walks slowly, and his shoes go
dop *dup* dop *dup*.

I can't hear my shoes. I wear sneakers.

I hear all sorts of sounds on a Listening Walk.

I listen to sounds I never listened to before.

I listen to lawn mowers.

Lawn mowers are noisy.

A lawn mower makes a steady zooming noise.

It goes like this:

z-z-z-z-z-zzzzzzooooooooooooooommmm.

I like to listen to lawn sprinklers.

Lawn sprinklers are very quiet.

They make different sounds.

Some sprinklers make a steady whispering sound like this: *thhhhhhhhhhhhhhhhhhh.*

Other sprinklers turn around and around.
They go like this:
whithhh *whithhh* *whithhh* *whithhh.*

On a Listening Walk I hear cars in the street.

The shiny new cars are quiet.

They make only a soft *hmmmmmmmmmm.*

But old cars are very noisy.

Old cars sound like this:

brack-a *brack-a* *brack-a* *brack-a.*

When cars go around the corner too fast,
the tires go *whhrrrrrrrrrrr.*

When cars stop quickly,
the brakes go

eeeeeeeeeeeeeeeeeee.

On a Listening Walk I hear all kinds of sounds —
a bicycle bell ringing:

trring   trring,

a baby crying:

waaaa

awaaaa

awaaaa

awaaaa.

A jet flies over.

Jets are very noisy when they're overhead.

A jet goes

eeeeeeeyowwwoooooooooooooooooo.

A boy runs by dribbling his basketball:

bomp   *bomp*

     bomp   *bomp.*

A lady hurries by us.

She is wearing high heels.

The lady's high heels go

bik   bik   bik
    bok   bok   bok.

A bus is coming.

The lady starts to run:

bik bik bik bik bik bik.

The bus stops at the corner:
pfsssss.
The lady gets on.

The bus starts up again:

chrrooooooooooooffff.

Around the corner men are digging up the street.

They are using a jackhammer.

It makes a loud banging sound:

dak-dak-dak-dak-dak-dak-dak.

The jackhammer hurts my ears.

I put my hands over my ears as we walk by:

dak-dak-dak-dak-dak-dak-dak.

19

Sometimes my father and I take Major to the park.

It is quiet there.

The sounds in the park are not loud like the noises in the street.

My father and I walk down a shady path.

I do not talk. I listen.

I listen to my father's shoes on the path.

They make a soft sound.

They go *chuff* *chuff* *chuff* *chuff.*

I listen to the birds in the park.

I listen to the pigeons and the ducks.

The pigeons fly down to meet us.

They want us to feed them.

The pigeons puff up their feathers.

They take little tiny steps.

They come toward us, nodding their heads.

They say *prrrooo*

prrrooo

prrrooo

prrrooo.

At the pond the ducks are waiting.

They want us to feed them, too.

The small ducks swim up close.

They turn their heads on one side and look up at us.

The small ducks waggle their tails and quack.

They say

gank gank   wonk wonk   gank gank.

The big ducks are not so brave.

They stay back and swim around in circles.

The big ducks look at us but they do not come close.

The big ducks say

gaaaaank   gaaaaank   gaaaaank.

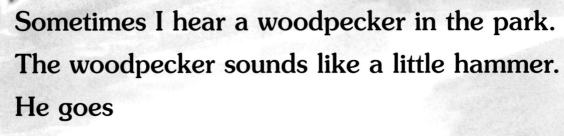

Sometimes I hear a woodpecker in the park.

The woodpecker sounds like a little hammer.

He goes

rat-tat-tat-tat-tat.

In the park I hear crickets in the grass.

The crickets go

creet

creet

creet.

I hear the wind in the leaves.
It whispers
　　　shhhhhh h h h h　h　h　h.

I hear bees in the flowers:
　　　bzzzzzzzzzzzzzzzz.

It is fun to go on a Listening Walk.

You do not have to go far.

You can walk around the block and listen.

You can walk around your yard and listen.

You do not even have to take a walk to hear sounds.

There are sounds everywhere all the time.

All you have to do is keep still and listen to them.

29

Right now there are sounds you can hear.

When you finish this page, close the book and listen.

How many different sounds can you hear right now?

Close your book and count them!

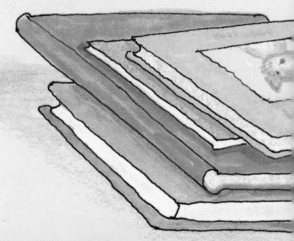